EASY
BAKE SALE
recipes

D1308433

Publications International, Ltd.
Favorite Brand Name Recipes at www.fbnr.com

Microwave Cooking: Microwave ovens vary in wattage. Use the cooking times as guidelines and check for doneness before adding more time.

Preparation/Cooking Times: Preparation times are based on the approximate amount of time required to assemble the recipe before cooking, baking, chilling or serving. These times include preparation steps such as measuring, chopping and mixing. The fact that some preparations and cooking can be done simultaneously is taken into account. Preparation of optional ingredients and serving suggestions is not included.

CONTENTS

TIPS FOR YOUR TREATS

HOLD IT!

• Foil pans can save on cleanup and eliminate the worry of lost pans. You can find foil pans with decorative prints at party supply stores.

• Paper "Chinese food" boxes can be used to hold caramel corn, snack mixes or small cookies.

• Attractive heavy-duty paper plates are a better-looking and more secure alternative to ordinary, flimsy paper plates.

LIVING LARGE

Brownies and bars will sell better if they are cut larger than usual and then individually wrapped.

Big cookies are also popular. Use $\frac{1}{4}$ cup of dough per cookie and extend baking time by a few minutes until cookies are done. This works best for oatmeal, chocolate chip, peanut butter and sugar cookies. Wrap these individually, too.

It's a Wrap

• Colored plastic wrap adds an eye-catching touch.

• After wrapping a loaf of quick bread with plastic wrap, place on a paper doily. Bring up the sides of the doily onto the long sides of the bread. Tie with a ribbon.

• Cellophane bags, clear or decorated, make simple work of wrapping small cookies or other tiny treats. Just fill and tie with ribbon or cord.

FOILED AGAIN

For bars and brownies, line pans with foil that extends 3 inches over the sides before proceeding with the recipe. Not only does this save on cleanup, it is also easier to cut equal-size bars when they are not in a pan.

Play It Safe

• Avoid selling cream-filled pastries, custards or other milk- and egg-based goodies.

• Use tongs or serving utensils to serve items that aren't individually wrapped.

• Always follow food safety precautions when preparing the food.

• Put labels on baked goods that contain ingredients like nuts, coconut or peanut butter since they can't always be readily seen. This will make it easier for people with allergies to select appropriate items.

HAVE CUPCAKES, WILL TRAVEL

Cupcakes can be difficult to transport without damaging the frosting. Solve this problem by placing them back in the muffin pans after they are cooled and frosted. Place toothpicks in the tops of some of the cupcakes and cover with plastic wrap or foil.

CAKE WALK DIRECTIONS

Looking for a fun way to raise money for your organization? Try a cake walk! It's a great addition to a school carnival or bazaar.

WHAT IS IT?

A cake walk is a group game in which the prize is a cake.

WHAT YOU NEED:

- 15 paper plates
- A marker
- Tape
- 15 slips of paper
- A hat or other container
- Fun music
- A medium- to large-size room
- Donated cakes (or other baked goods, if you wish)
- People who want to have fun and win cake

HOW TO GET READY:

• Clear a large space in the middle of the room.

• Write the numbers 1 through 15 on the paper plates with the marker. Tape the plates securely to the floor in numerical order in a large circle, allowing about 1 foot between plates.

• Write the numbers 1 through 15 on slips of paper; fold them and place in the hat.

• Cue up the music.

HOW TO PLAY:

1. Collect the money. Determine beforehand what you want to charge, usually between 25¢ and 50¢.

2. When you have enough people to play (about 8 to 15 people), explain how the game works.

3. Have each person stand on a number.

4. Start the music. Let it play for about the amount of time it takes to go around the circle twice.

5. Stop the music. Everyone stops on the closest number, one person to a number.

6. Draw a number from the hat. Whoever is on that number wins their choice of the donated cakes.

7. Return the number to the hat. Repeat with a new group of people until you run out of prizes.

Golden Gingersnaps

1 package DUNCAN HINES® Golden Sugar Cookie Mix
1 egg
1 tablespoon water
1 tablespoon light molasses
1½ teaspoons ground ginger
1 teaspoon ground cinnamon
½ teaspoon baking soda
¼ cup granulated sugar
1 tablespoon milk
⅓ cup finely chopped pecans

Preheat oven to 375°F. Grease cookie sheets.

Combine cookie mix, egg, water, molasses, ginger, cinnamon and baking soda in large bowl. Stir until thoroughly blended. Drop by level tablespoonfuls into sugar. Roll to completely cover. Place 2 inches apart onto prepared cookie sheets. Flatten slightly with bottom of drinking glass. Brush tops lightly with milk. Sprinkle with pecans. Bake 9 minutes for chewy cookies or 10 minutes for crisp cookies. Cool 2 minutes on cookie sheets. Remove to cooling racks. Cool completely. Store in airtight container.

Makes 3 dozen cookies

Allow cookie sheets to cool between batches because the dough will spread if it is placed on a hot cookie sheet.

Golden Gingersnaps

Three-in-One Chocolate Chip Cookies

....

6 tablespoons butter or
   margarine, softened
½ cup packed light brown
   sugar
¼ cup granulated sugar
1 egg
1 teaspoon vanilla extract
1½ cups all-purpose flour
½ teaspoon baking soda
¼ teaspoon salt
2 cups (12-ounce package)
   HERSHEY₃S Semi-
   Sweet Chocolate Chips

Beat butter, brown sugar and granulated sugar in large bowl until light and fluffy. Add egg and vanilla; beat well. Stir together flour, baking soda and salt; gradually blend into butter mixture. Stir in chocolate chips. Shape and bake cookies into one of the three versions below.

Giant Cookie: Prepare dough. Heat oven to 350°F. Line 12×⅝-inch round pizza pan with foil. Pat dough evenly into prepared pan to within ¾-inch of edge. Bake 15 to 18 minutes or until lightly browned. Cool; cut into wedges.
Makes about 8 servings (one 12-inch cookie)

Medium-Size Refrigerator Cookies: Prepare dough. On wax paper, shape into 2 rolls, 1½ inches in diameter. Wrap in wax paper; cover with plastic wrap. Refrigerate several hours, or until firm enough to slice. Heat oven to 350°F. Remove rolls from refrigerator; remove wrapping. With sharp knife, cut into ¼-inch-wide slices. Place on ungreased cookie sheet, about 3 inches apart. Bake 8 to 10 minutes or until lightly browned. Cool slightly; remove from cookie sheet to wire rack. Cool completely.
Makes about 2½ dozen cookies (2½ inches)

Miniature Cookies: Prepare dough. Heat oven to 350°F. Drop dough by ¼ teaspoonfuls onto ungreased cookie sheet, about 1½ inches apart. (Or spoon dough into disposable plastic frosting bag; cut about ¼ inch off tip. Squeeze batter by ¼ teaspoonfuls onto ungreased cookie sheet.) Bake 5 to 7 minutes or just until set. Cool slightly; remove from cookie sheet to wire rack. Cool completely.
Makes about 18½ dozen cookies (¾ inch)

Giant Three-in-One Chocolate Chip Cookie

Domino Cookies

1 package (20 ounces)
  refrigerated sugar
  cookie dough,
  unwrapped
All-purpose flour
  (optional)
½ cup semisweet chocolate
  chips

1. Preheat oven to 350°F. Grease cookie sheets.

2. Cut dough into 4 equal sections. Reserve 1 section; refrigerate remaining 3 sections.

3. Roll reserved dough to ⅛-inch thickness. Sprinkle with flour to minimize sticking, if necessary.

4. Cut out 9 (2½×1¾-inch) rectangles using sharp knife. Place 2 inches apart on prepared cookie sheets.

5. Score each cookie across middle with sharp knife.

6. Gently press chips, point sides down, into dough to resemble dominos. Repeat with remaining dough and scraps.

7. Bake 8 to 10 minutes or until edges are light golden brown. Remove to wire racks; cool.
Makes 3 dozen cookies

Simpler Than Sin Peanut Chocolate Cookies

1 cup PETER PAN® Extra
  Crunchy Peanut Butter
1 cup sugar
1 egg, at room
  temperature and
  beaten
2 teaspoons vanilla
1 (6-ounce) dark or milk
  chocolate candy bar,
  broken into squares

Preheat oven to 350°F. In a medium bowl, combine Peter Pan® Peanut Butter, sugar, egg, and vanilla; mix well. Roll dough into 1-inch balls. Place 2 inches apart on ungreased cookie sheet. Bake 12 minutes. Remove from oven and place chocolate square in center of each cookie. Bake an additional 5 to 7 minutes or until cookies are lightly golden around edges. Cool 5 minutes. Remove to wire rack. Cool.
Makes 21 to 24 cookies

Note: This simple recipe is unusual because it doesn't contain any flour—but it still makes great cookies!

Domino Cookies

Cranberry Brown Sugar Cookies

- 2 cups firmly packed DOMINO® Dark Brown Sugar
- 1 cup butter or margarine, softened
- 2 eggs
- ½ cup sour cream
- 3½ cups all-purpose flour
- 1 teaspoon baking soda
- 1 teaspoon salt
- 1 teaspoon ground cinnamon
- ½ teaspoon ground nutmeg
- ¼ teaspoon ground cloves
- 1 cup dried cranberries (5 ounces)
- 1 cup golden raisins

Heat oven to 400°F. Lightly grease cookie sheets. Beat sugar and butter in large bowl until light and fluffy. Add eggs and sour cream; beat until creamy. Stir together flour, baking soda, salt, cinnamon, nutmeg and cloves in small bowl; gradually add to sugar mixture, beating until well mixed. Stir in cranberries and raisins. Drop by rounded teaspoonfuls onto cookie sheets. Bake 8 to 10 minutes or until lightly browned. Remove from cookie sheets to cooling racks. Cool.

Makes about 5 dozen cookies

Reduced Fat Version: Substitute 70% spread margarine for butter, ½ cup refrigerated or frozen nonfat egg product, thawed, for the 2 eggs, and nonfat sour cream for the sour cream. Proceed as directed. Per cookie: 87 calories, 2 g fat.

Tips: 1 cup chopped dried cherries may be substituted for 1 cup dried cranberries. If cranberries are exceptionally large, chop before adding to cookie dough.

Preparation Time: 30 minutes
Bake Time: 10 minutes
Cooling Time: 30 minutes

To quickly soften butter or margarine, remove wrapper and place butter on a microwavable plate. Microwave at LOW (30% power) for 20 to 30 seconds for one stick.

Chewy Lemon-Honey Cookies

2 cups all-purpose flour
1½ teaspoons baking soda
½ cup honey
⅓ cup FLEISCHMANN'S®
   Original Margarine
¼ cup granulated sugar
1 tablespoon grated lemon
   peel
¼ cup EGG BEATERS®
   Healthy Real Egg
   Product
Lemon Glaze, optional
   (recipe follows)

In small bowl, combine flour and baking soda; set aside.

In large bowl, with electric mixer at medium speed, beat honey, margarine, granulated sugar and lemon peel until creamy. Add Egg Beaters®; beat until smooth. Gradually stir in flour mixture until blended.

Drop dough by rounded teaspoonfuls, 2 inches apart, onto lightly greased baking sheets. Bake at 350°F for 7 to 8 minutes or until lightly browned. Remove from sheets; cool completely on wire racks. Drizzle with Lemon Glaze, if desired.

Makes 3½ dozen cookies

Lemon Glaze: In small bowl, combine 1 cup powdered sugar and 2 tablespoons lemon juice until smooth.

Prep Time: 20 minutes
Bake Time: 8 minutes

6 ingredients or less!

Polka Dot Macaroons

1 14-ounce bag (5 cups)
   shredded coconut
1 14-ounce can sweetened
   condensed milk
½ cup all-purpose flour
1¾ cups "M&M's"®
   Chocolate Mini Baking
   Bits

Preheat oven to 350°F. Grease cookie sheets; set aside. In large bowl combine coconut, condensed milk and flour until well blended. Stir in "M&M's"® Chocolate Mini Baking Bits. Drop by rounded tablespoonfuls about 2 inches apart onto prepared cookie sheets. Bake 8 to 10 minutes or until edges are golden. Cool completely on wire racks. Store in tightly covered container.

Makes about 5 dozen cookies

6 ingredients or less!

Chocolate Macadamia Cookies

1 package DUNCAN
    HINES® Chocolate
    Chip Cookie Mix
¼ cup unsweetened cocoa
    powder
⅓ cup vegetable oil
1 egg
3 tablespoons water
⅔ cup coarsely chopped
    macadamia nuts

Preheat oven to 375°F.

Combine cookie mix and cocoa in large bowl. Add oil, egg and water. Stir until thoroughly blended. Stir in macadamia nuts. Drop by rounded teaspoonfuls 2 inches apart onto *ungreased* cookie sheets.

Bake 8 to 10 minutes or until set. Cool 1 minute on cookie sheets. Remove to cooling racks. Cool completely.

Makes 3 dozen cookies

San Francisco Cookies

2 extra-ripe, medium
    DOLE® Bananas, cut
    into chunks
2 cups granola
1½ cups all-purpose flour
1 cup packed brown sugar
1 teaspoon baking powder
1 teaspoon ground
    cinnamon
2 eggs
½ cup margarine, melted
¼ cup vegetable oil
1 cup chocolate chips

• Preheat oven to 350°F. Lightly grease cookie sheets. In food processor or blender, process bananas until puréed (1 cup).

• Combine granola, flour, sugar, baking powder and cinnamon in large bowl. Beat in puréed bananas, eggs, margarine and oil. Stir in chocolate chips.

• Drop by ¼ cupfuls onto prepared cookie sheets. Spread dough into 2½- to 3-inch circles. Bake about 16 minutes or until golden. Remove to wire racks to cool.

Makes about 16 cookies

Chocolate Macadamia Cookies

Molasses Oatmeal Cookies

1 Butter Flavor* CRISCO® Stick or 1 cup Butter Flavor CRISCO® all-vegetable shortening plus additional for greasing
1 cup firmly packed brown sugar
1 cup granulated sugar
2 eggs
1 tablespoon milk
1 tablespoon light molasses
2 teaspoons vanilla
2 cups all-purpose flour
1½ teaspoons cinnamon
1 teaspoon baking soda
½ teaspoon baking powder
½ teaspoon ground cloves
¼ teaspoon salt
2 cups quick oats (not instant or old fashioned)
1 cup coarsely chopped pecans
½ cup raisins

Butter Flavor Crisco is artificially flavored.

1. Heat oven to 350°F. Grease baking sheet with shortening. Place sheets of foil on countertop for cooling cookies.

2. Combine shortening, brown sugar, granulated sugar, eggs, milk, molasses and vanilla in large bowl. Beat at medium speed of electric mixer until well blended.

3. Combine flour, cinnamon, baking soda, baking powder, cloves and salt. Stir into creamed mixture with spoon until well blended. Stir in oats, nuts and raisins.

4. Form dough into 1-inch balls. Place 2 inches apart on baking sheet.

5. Bake at 350°F for 11 to 12 minutes, or until edges are lightly browned. *Do not overbake.* Cool 2 minutes on baking sheet. Remove cookies to foil to cool completely.

Makes about 4 dozen cookies

Apple Pie Wedges

1 cup butter, softened
⅔ cup sugar
⅓ cup apple butter
1 egg yolk
2⅓ cups all-purpose flour
1 teaspoon ground cinnamon
½ teaspoon apple pie spice
½ teaspoon vanilla

1. Beat butter and sugar in medium bowl at medium speed of electric mixer until fluffy.

2. Add apple butter and egg yolk; mix well. Add flour, cinnamon, apple pie spice and vanilla; beat at low speed until well blended.

3. Divide dough in half. Shape each half into a 6-inch disc on waxed paper. Refrigerate 30 minutes.

4. Preheat oven to 325°F. Invert 1 disc of dough into ungreased 9-inch round pie plate.

5. Press dough into plate with lightly floured hand, covering plate completely.

6. Flute edges using handle of wooden spoon. Deeply score into 8 wedges.

7. Prick surface using tines of fork. Repeat steps with remaining disc of dough and another pie plate.

8. Bake 35 minutes or until golden brown. Remove to wire rack; cool completely. Cut into wedges.   *Makes 16 wedges*

Tip: Serve these tasty cookies warm with a big scoop of vanilla or cinnamon-flavored ice cream.

Ranger Cookies

1 cup (2 sticks) margarine or butter, softened
1 cup granulated sugar
1 cup firmly packed brown sugar
2 eggs
1 teaspoon vanilla
2 cups all-purpose flour
1 teaspoon baking soda
½ teaspoon baking powder
½ teaspoon salt (optional)
2 cups QUAKER® Oats (quick or old fashioned, uncooked)
2 cups cornflakes
½ cup flaked or shredded coconut
½ cup chopped nuts

Heat oven to 350°F. Beat margarine and sugars until creamy. Add eggs and vanilla; beat well. Add combined flour, baking soda, baking powder and salt; mix well. Stir in oats, cornflakes, coconut and nuts; mix well. Drop dough by heaping tablespoonfuls onto ungreased cookie sheets. Bake 10 to 12 minutes or until light golden brown. Cool 1 minute on cookie sheets; remove to wire rack. Cool completely. Store tightly covered.
Makes 2 dozen large cookies

Happy Cookie Pops

1½ cups granulated sugar
1 cup butter-flavored solid
    vegetable shortening
2 large eggs
1 teaspoon vanilla extract
2¾ cups all-purpose flour
1 teaspoon baking powder
½ teaspoon baking soda
1¾ cups "M&M's"®
    Chocolate Mini Baking
    Bits, divided
    Additional granulated
    sugar
2½ dozen flat wooden ice
    cream sticks
    Prepared frostings
    Tubes of decorator's
    icing

In large bowl cream 1½ cups sugar and shortening until light and fluffy; beat in eggs and vanilla. In medium bowl combine flour, baking powder and baking soda; blend into creamed mixture. Stir in 1¼ cups "M&M's"® Chocolate Mini Baking Bits. Wrap and refrigerate dough 1 hour.

Preheat oven to 375°F. Roll 1½ tablespoons dough into ball and roll in granulated sugar. Insert ice cream stick into each ball. Place about 2 inches apart onto ungreased cookie sheets; gently flatten, using bottom of small plate. On half the cookies, make a smiling face by placing some of the remaining "M&M's"® Chocolate Mini Baking Bits on the surface; leave other cookies for decorating after baking. Bake all cookies 10 to 12 minutes or until golden. Cool 2 minutes on cookie sheets; cool completely on wire racks. Decorate cookies as desired using frostings, decorator's icing and remaining "M&M's"® Chocolate Mini Baking Bits. Store in single layer in tightly covered container.
Makes 2½ dozen cookies

Happy Cookie Pops

Mini Kisses Coconut Macaroon Bars

3¾ cups (10-ounce package) MOUNDS® Sweetened Coconut Flakes
¾ cup sugar
¼ cup all-purpose flour
¼ teaspoon salt
3 egg whites
1 whole egg, slightly beaten
1 teaspoon almond extract
1 cup HERSHEY'S MINI KISSES® Milk Chocolate Baking Pieces

1. Heat oven to 350°F. Lightly grease 9-inch square baking pan.

2. Stir together coconut, sugar, flour and salt in large bowl. Add egg whites, whole egg and almond extract; stir until well blended. Stir in MINI KISSES. Spread mixture into prepared pan, covering all chocolate pieces with coconut mixture.

3. Bake 35 minutes or until lightly browned. Cool completely in pan on wire rack. Cover with foil; allow to stand at room temperature about 8 hours or overnight. Cut into bars.

Makes about 24 bars

Variation: Omit MINI KISSES in batter. Immediately after removing pan from oven, place desired number of chocolate pieces on top, pressing down lightly. Cool completely. Cut into bars.

Prep Time: 15 minutes
Bake Time: 35 minutes
Cool Time: 9 hours

Mini Kisses Coconut Macaroon Bars

Lemon Bars

1 package DUNCAN
   HINES® Moist Deluxe
   Lemon Supreme Cake
   Mix
3 eggs, divided
⅓ cup butter-flavor
   shortening
½ cup granulated sugar
¼ cup lemon juice
2 teaspoons grated lemon
   peel
½ teaspoon baking powder
¼ teaspoon salt
   Confectioners' sugar

Preheat oven to 350°F.

Combine cake mix, 1 egg and
shortening in large mixing bowl.
Beat at low speed with electric
mixer until crumbs form. Reserve
1 cup. Pat remaining mixture
lightly into *ungreased* 13×9-
inch pan. Bake 15 minutes or
until lightly browned.

Combine remaining 2 eggs,
granulated sugar, lemon juice,
lemon peel, baking powder and
salt in medium mixing bowl. Beat
at medium speed with electric
mixer until light and foamy. Pour
over hot crust. Sprinkle with
reserved crumb mixture.

Bake 15 minutes or until lightly
browned. Sprinkle with
confectioners' sugar. Cool in
pan. Cut into bars.

Makes 30 to 32 bars

Tip: These bars are also delicious
using DUNCAN HINES® Moist
Deluxe Yellow Cake Mix.

Fudgy Chip Bars

50 OREO® Chocolate
   Sandwich Cookies,
   coarsely crushed
1 cup flaked coconut
1 cup semisweet chocolate
   chips
¼ cup margarine or butter,
   melted
1 (14-ounce) can
   sweetened condensed
   milk
1 teaspoon vanilla extract

In medium bowl, combine
cookies, coconut and chocolate
chips. Stir in margarine or butter,
condensed milk and vanilla
extract. Spread into greased
9×9×2-inch baking pan. Bake
at 375°F for 30 minutes or until
done. Cool and cut into bars.

Makes 2 dozen bars

Lemon Bars

Chocolate Caramel Brownies

1 package (18¼ to 18½ ounces) devil's food or chocolate cake mix
1 cup chopped nuts
½ cup (1 stick) butter or margarine, melted
1 cup *undiluted* CARNATION® Evaporated Milk, divided
35 light caramels (10 ounces)
1 cup (6-ounce package) NESTLÉ® TOLL HOUSE® Semi-Sweet Chocolate Morsels

COMBINE cake mix and nuts in large bowl; stir in butter. Stir in *½ cup* evaporated milk (batter will be thick). Spread half of batter in greased 13×9-inch baking pan.

BAKE in preheated 350°F. oven for 15 minutes.

COMBINE caramels and *remaining* evaporated milk in small saucepan; cook over low heat, stirring occasionally, until caramels are melted. Sprinkle morsels over baked layer. Drizzle melted caramels over chocolate morsels, carefully spreading to cover chocolate layer. Drop remaining half of batter in heaping teaspoons over caramel mixture.

RETURN to oven; bake 20 to 25 minutes longer (top layer will be soft). Cool completely before cutting.   *Makes 48 brownies*

Cranberry Walnut Bars

Bar Cookie Crust (recipe follows)
2 eggs
½ cup KARO® Light or Dark Corn Syrup
½ cup sugar
2 tablespoons MAZOLA® Margarine, melted
1 cup dried cranberries or raisins
¾ cup chopped walnuts

1. Preheat oven to 350°F. Prepare Bar Cookie Crust according to recipe directions.

2. In large bowl beat eggs, corn syrup, sugar and margarine until well blended. Stir in cranberries and walnuts. Pour over hot crust; spread evenly.

3. Bake 15 to 18 minutes or until set. Cool completely on wire rack before cutting. Cut into 2×1½-inch bars.

Makes 32 bars

Prep Time: 30 minutes
Bake Time: 15 to 18 minutes, plus cooling

Bar Cookie Crust

MAZOLA NO STICK®
Cooking Spray
2 cups flour
½ cup (1 stick) cold MAZOLA® Margarine or butter, cut into pieces
⅓ cup sugar
¼ teaspoon salt

1. Preheat oven to 350°F. Spray 13×9×2-inch baking pan with cooking spray.

2. In large bowl with mixer at medium speed, beat flour, margarine, sugar and salt until mixture resembles coarse crumbs. Press firmly into bottom and ¼ inch up sides of prepared pan.

3. Bake 15 minutes or until golden brown. Top with filling. Complete as recipe directs.

Prep Time: 10 minutes
Bake Time: 15 minutes

Oat-Y Nut Bars

½ cup butter
½ cup honey
¼ cup packed brown sugar
¼ cup corn syrup
2¾ cups uncooked quick oats
⅔ cup raisins
½ cup salted peanuts

Preheat oven to 300°F. Grease 9-inch square baking pan. Melt butter with honey, brown sugar and corn syrup in medium saucepan over medium heat, stirring constantly. Bring to a boil; boil 8 minutes or until mixture thickens slightly. Stir in oats, raisins and peanuts until well blended. Press evenly into prepared pan.

Bake 45 to 50 minutes or until golden brown. Place pan on wire rack; score top into 2-inch squares. Cool completely. Cut into bars. *Makes 16 bars*

Peanut Butter Chip Triangles

1½ cups all-purpose flour
½ cup packed light brown sugar
½ cup (1 stick) cold butter or margarine
1⅔ cups (10-ounce package) REESE'S® Peanut Butter Chips, divided
1 can (14 ounces) sweetened condensed milk (not evaporated milk)
1 egg, slightly beaten
1 teaspoon vanilla extract
¾ cup chopped walnuts
Powdered sugar (optional)

1. Heat oven to 350°F. Stir together flour and brown sugar in medium bowl. Cut in butter with pastry blender or fork until mixture resembles coarse crumbs. Stir in ½ cup peanut butter chips. Press mixture into bottom of ungreased 13×9×2-inch baking pan. Bake 15 minutes.

2. Meanwhile, combine sweetened condensed milk, egg and vanilla in large bowl. Stir in remaining chips and walnuts. Spread evenly over hot baked crust.

3. Bake 25 minutes or until golden brown. Cool completely in pan on wire rack. Cut into 2- or 2½-inch squares; cut squares diagonally into triangles. Sift powdered sugar over top, if desired.

Makes 24 or 40 triangles

Tip: To sprinkle powdered sugar over brownies, bars, cupcakes or other desserts, place sugar in a wire mesh strainer. Hold over top of desserts and gently tap sides of strainer.

Prep Time: 20 minutes
Bake Time: 40 minutes
Cool Time: 2 hours

Peanut Butter Chip Triangles

German Chocolate Brownies

1 package DUNCAN HINES® Milk Chocolate Chunk Brownie Mix
2 eggs
⅓ cup water
⅓ cup vegetable oil
½ cup packed brown sugar
2 tablespoons butter or margarine, softened
1 tablespoon all-purpose flour
½ cup chopped pecans
½ cup flaked coconut

Preheat oven to 350°F. Grease bottom only of 13×9-inch pan.

Combine brownie mix, eggs, water and oil in large bowl. Stir with spoon until well blended, about 50 strokes. Spread into prepared pan.

Combine sugar, butter and flour in small bowl. Mix until well blended. Stir in pecans and coconut. Sprinkle mixture over batter. Bake 25 to 30 minutes or until topping is browned. Cool completely in pan. Cut into bars.
Makes 24 brownies

Tip: Always mix brownies by hand. Never use an electric mixer.

Hershey's Syrup Snacking Brownies

½ cup (1 stick) butter or margarine, softened
1 cup sugar
1½ cups (16-ounce can) HERSHEY'S Syrup
4 eggs
1¼ cups all-purpose flour
1 cup HERSHEY'S Semi-Sweet Chocolate Chips

1. Heat oven to 350°F. Grease 13×9×2-inch baking pan.

2. Beat butter and sugar in large bowl. Add syrup, eggs and flour; beat well. Stir in chocolate chips. Pour batter into prepared pan.

3. Bake 30 to 35 minutes or until brownies begin to pull away from sides of pan. Cool completely in pan on wire rack. Cut into bars.
Makes about 36 brownies

Caramel Apple Bars

CRUST
- ¾ Butter Flavor* CRISCO® Stick or ¾ cup Butter Flavor CRISCO® all-vegetable shortening plus additional for greasing
- 1 cup firmly packed light brown sugar
- 1 egg
- 1½ cups all-purpose flour
- ½ teaspoon salt
- ½ teaspoon baking soda
- 1¾ cups quick oats, uncooked

FILLING
- 3 to 4 Granny Smith or Golden Delicious apples, peeled and cut into ½-inch dice (about 4 cups)
- 2 tablespoons all-purpose flour
- 1 teaspoon lemon juice
- 1 bag (14 ounces) caramel candy, unwrapped

*Butter Flavor Crisco is artificially flavored.

1. Heat oven to 350°F. Grease 13×9×2-inch baking pan with shortening.

2. For crust, combine shortening and brown sugar in large bowl. Beat at medium speed of electric mixer. Add egg to creamed mixture. Beat until well blended.

3. Combine 1½ cups flour, salt and baking soda. Add to creamed mixture gradually. Add in oats. Mix until blended. Reserve 1¼ cups of mixture for topping. Press remaining mixture into prepared pan.

4. Bake at 350°F for 10 minutes.

5. For filling, toss apples with 2 tablespoons flour and lemon juice. Distribute apple mixture evenly over partially baked crust. Press in lightly.

6. Place caramels in microwave-safe bowl. Microwave at HIGH (100%) for 1 minute. Stir. Repeat until caramels are melted. Drizzle melted caramel evenly over apples. Crumble reserved topping evenly over caramel.

7. Bake at 350°F for 30 to 40 minutes, or until apples are tender and top is golden brown. *Do not overbake.* Loosen caramel from sides of pan with knife. Cool completely. Cut into about 1½-inch bars. Cover tightly with plastic wrap to store.
Makes about 4 dozen bars

Chocolate Marbled Blondies

½ cup (1 stick) butter or
  margarine, softened
½ cup firmly packed light
  brown sugar
1 large egg
2 teaspoons vanilla extract
1½ cups all-purpose flour
1¼ teaspoons baking soda
1 cup "M&M's"® Chocolate
  Mini Baking Bits,
  divided
4 ounces cream cheese,
  softened
2 tablespoons granulated
  sugar
1 large egg yolk
¼ cup unsweetened cocoa
  powder

Preheat oven to 350°F. Lightly
grease 9×9×2-inch baking pan;
set aside. In large bowl cream
butter and brown sugar until light
and fluffy; beat in egg and
vanilla. In medium bowl combine
flour and baking soda; blend into
creamed mixture. Stir in ⅔ cup
"M&M's"® Chocolate Mini
Baking Bits; set aside. *Dough
will be stiff.* In separate bowl
beat together cream cheese,
granulated sugar and egg yolk
until smooth; stir in cocoa
powder until well blended. Place
chocolate-cheese mixture in six
equal portions evenly onto

bottom of prepared pan. Place
reserved dough around cheese
mixture and swirl slightly with
tines of fork. Pat down evenly on
top. Sprinkle with remaining ⅓
cup "M&M's"® Chocolate Mini
Baking Bits. Bake 25 to 30
minutes or until toothpick
inserted in center comes out with
moist crumbs. Cool completely.
Cut into bars. Store in
refrigerator in tightly covered
container.   *Makes 16 bars*

To soften cream
cheese, remove wrapper
and place cream cheese on
a microwavable plate.
Microwave at MEDIUM (50%
power) for 1 to 1½ minutes
for an 8-ounce package or
30 to 45 seconds for a
3-ounce package.

Chocolate Marbled Blondies

Rocky Road Brownies

½ cup butter
½ cup unsweetened cocoa
1 cup sugar
½ cup all-purpose flour
¼ cup buttermilk
1 egg
1 teaspoon vanilla
1 cup miniature
    marshmallows
1 cup coarsely chopped
    walnuts
1 cup (6 ounces) semisweet
    chocolate chips

Preheat oven to 350°F. Lightly grease 8-inch square pan. Combine butter and cocoa in medium saucepan over low heat, stirring constantly until smooth. Remove from heat; stir in sugar, flour, buttermilk, egg and vanilla. Mix until smooth. Spread batter evenly in prepared pan. Bake 25 minutes or until center feels dry. (Do not overbake or brownies will be dry.) Remove from oven; sprinkle marshmallows, walnuts and chocolate chips over the top. Return to oven for 3 to 5 minutes or just until topping is warmed enough to meld. Cool in pan on wire rack. Cut into 2-inch squares.

Makes 16 brownies

Nuggets o' Gold Brownies

3 ounces unsweetened
    baking chocolate
¼ cup WESSON® Vegetable
    Oil
2 eggs
1 cup sugar
1 teaspoon vanilla extract
¼ teaspoon salt
½ cup all-purpose flour
1 (3.8-ounce)
    BUTTERFINGER®
    Candy Bar, coarsely
    chopped

In microwave-safe measuring cup, heat chocolate 2 minutes on HIGH in microwave oven. Stir and continue heating in 30-second intervals until chocolate is completely melted. Stir in oil and set aside to cool. In mixing bowl, beat eggs until foamy. Whisk in sugar, then add vanilla and salt. Stir in chocolate mixture, then mix in flour until all ingredients are moistened. Gently fold in candy. Pour batter into 9-inch greased baking pan and bake at 350°F for 25 to 30 minutes or until edges begin to pull away from sides of pan. Cool before cutting.

Makes 20 brownies

Rocky Road Brownies

PAGEANT
OF PIES

Blueberry Crumble Pie

1 KEEBLER® Ready Crust® Graham Cracker Pie Crust
1 egg yolk, beaten
1 (21-ounce) can blueberry pie filling
⅓ cup all-purpose flour
⅓ cup quick-cooking oats
¼ cup sugar
3 tablespoons margarine, melted

Preheat oven to 375°F. Brush bottom and sides of crust with egg yolk; bake on baking sheet until light brown, about 5 minutes.

Pour blueberry pie filling into crust. In small bowl, combine flour, oats and sugar; mix in melted margarine. Spoon over pie filling.

Bake on baking sheet about 35 minutes or until filling is bubbly and topping is browned.

Makes 1 pie

Prep Time: 15 minutes
Bake Time: 40 minutes

Brushing egg yolk on the crust before baking "seals" the crust and prevents it from getting soggy from the moisture in the filling.

Blueberry Crumble Pie

Apple Almond Pie

¾ cup sugar, divided
¼ cup ARGO® or
      KINGSFORD'S® Corn
      Starch
 3 eggs
½ cup (1 stick) MAZOLA®
      Margarine, melted
½ cup KARO® Light or
      Dark Corn Syrup
¼ teaspoon almond extract
 2 cups peeled, chopped
      apples (about 2 large)
 1 cup sliced or slivered
      almonds, toasted
      Easy-As-Pie Crust
      (recipe follows),
      unbaked
 1 apple, peeled and thinly
      sliced (optional)
      Sliced almonds, toasted
      (optional)

1. Preheat oven to 375°F.
Reserve 2 tablespoons sugar.

2. In medium bowl combine
remaining sugar and corn starch.
Beat in eggs until well blended.
Stir in margarine, corn syrup and
almond extract.

3. Mix in chopped apples and
almonds. Pour into pie crust.

4. If desired, garnish with apple
slices arranged in a circle around
edge of pie; fill center of circle
with additional toasted almonds.
Sprinkle reserved sugar over top.

5. Bake 50 minutes or until
puffed and set. Cool on wire
rack.   *Makes 8 servings*

Note: All-purpose apples such
as Gravenstein, Jonathan,
McIntosh or Winesap are ideal
for this pie. If you prefer a
cooking apple, try Northern Spy,
Greening or Rome Beauty, but
add a few minutes to the baking
time.

Prep Time: 20 minutes
Bake Time: 50 minutes, plus
cooling

EASY-AS-PIE CRUST

1¼ cups unsifted flour
 ⅛ teaspoon salt
 ½ cup MAZOLA® Margarine
 2 to 3 tablespoons cold
      water

1. In medium bowl, combine
flour and salt. With pastry blender
or 2 knives, cut in margarine until
mixture resembles fine crumbs.

2. Sprinkle water over mixture
while tossing to blend well. Press
dough firmly into ball.

3. On lightly floured surface, roll
into 12-inch circle. Fit loosely into
9-inch pie plate. Trim and flute
edge. Fill and bake according to
recipe.

Makes 1 (9-inch) crust

Triple Berry Pie

1½ cups raspberries
1½ cups strawberries, sliced
1 cup blueberries
1 baked pastry shell (9 inch), cooled
¾ cup sugar
3 tablespoons cornstarch
1½ cups water
1 package (4-serving size) JELL-O® Brand Strawberry Flavor Gelatin
1 tub (8 ounces) COOL WHIP® Whipped Topping, thawed
Fresh mint leaves

STIR berries together in large bowl. Place in pastry shell.

MIX sugar and cornstarch in medium saucepan. Gradually stir in water until smooth. Stirring constantly, bring to boil on medium heat; boil 1 minute. Remove from heat. Stir in gelatin until completely dissolved. Cool to room temperature; pour over berries in pastry shell.

REFRIGERATE 3 hours or until firm. Spread whipped topping over pie just before serving.

Makes 8 servings

Luscious Brownie Chip Pie

25 CHIPS AHOY!® Chocolate Chip Cookies
½ cup margarine or butter, melted, divided
½ cup light corn syrup
3 eggs
½ cup sugar
⅓ cup unsweetened cocoa
2 teaspoons vanilla extract
Whipped cream and chocolate curls for garnish

Cut 5 cookies in half; set aside. Roll remaining cookies between two pieces of waxed paper until fine crumbs form. Combine crumbs and ¼ cup margarine or butter; press on bottom and up side of 9-inch pie plate.

In saucepan, heat remaining ¼ cup margarine or butter and corn syrup until warm; remove from heat. Beat in eggs, sugar, cocoa and vanilla; pour into crust. Bake at 350°F 15 minutes; insert cookie halves around edge of pie crust. Bake 15 to 20 minutes more or until set, tenting with foil during last 5 to 10 minutes if excessive browning occurs. Cool. Garnish.

Makes 8 servings

White Chocolate Cranberry Tart

1 refrigerated pie crust
    (half of a 15-ounce
    package)
1 cup sugar
2 eggs
¼ cup butter or margarine,
    melted
2 teaspoons vanilla
½ cup all-purpose flour
1 package (6 ounces) white
    chocolate baking bar,
    chopped
½ cup chopped macadamia
    nuts, lightly toasted*
½ cup dried cranberries,
    coarsely chopped

*Toast chopped macadamia nuts in hot skillet about 3 minutes or until fragrant.

1. Preheat oven to 350°F. Line 9-inch tart pan with removable bottom or pie pan with pie crust (refrigerate or freeze other crust for another use).

2. Combine sugar, eggs, butter and vanilla in large bowl; mix well. Stir in flour until well blended. Add white chocolate, nuts and cranberries.

3. Pour filling into prepared pan. Bake 50 to 55 minutes or until top of tart is crusty and deep golden brown and knife inserted in center comes out clean.

4. Cool completely on wire rack. Cover and store at room temperature until serving time. Garnish as desired.

Makes 8 servings

Spraying your knife with nonstick cooking spray before chopping dried cranberries will prevent them from sticking to the knife.

White Chocolate
Cranberry Tart

Cider Apple Pie in Cheddar Crust

CRUST
- 2 cups sifted all-purpose flour
- 1 cup shredded Cheddar cheese
- ½ teaspoon salt
- ⅔ CRISCO® Stick or ⅔ cup CRISCO® all-vegetable shortening
- 5 to 6 tablespoons ice water

FILLING
- 6 cups sliced, peeled apples (about 2 pounds or 6 medium)
- 1 cup apple cider
- ⅔ cup sugar
- 2 tablespoons cornstarch
- 2 tablespoons water
- ½ teaspoon cinnamon
- 1 tablespoon butter or margarine

GLAZE
- 1 egg yolk
- 1 tablespoon water

1. Heat oven to 400°F.

2. For crust, place flour, cheese and salt in food processor bowl. Add shortening. Process 15 seconds. Sprinkle water through food chute, 1 tablespoon at a time, until dough just forms (process time not to exceed 20 seconds). Shape into ball; divide in half. Press to form two 5- to 6-inch "pancakes." Roll and press bottom crust into 9-inch pie plate.

3. For filling, combine apples, apple cider and sugar in large saucepan. Cook and stir on medium-high heat until mixture comes to a boil. Reduce heat to low. Simmer 5 minutes. Combine cornstarch, water and cinnamon. Stir into apples. Cook and stir until mixture comes to a boil. Remove from heat. Stir in butter. Spoon into pie crust. Moisten pastry edge with water.

4. Roll top crust. Lift onto filled pie. Trim ½ inch beyond edge of pie plate. Fold top edge under bottom crust. Flute. Cut slits or design in top crust to allow steam to escape.

5. For glaze, beat egg yolk with fork in small bowl. Stir in water. Brush over top.

6. Bake at 400°F for 35 to 40 minutes or until filling in center is bubbly and crust is golden brown. Cover edge with foil, if necessary, to prevent overbrowning. *Do not overbake.* Cool.

Makes 1 (9-inch) pie

Cider Apple Pie
in Cheddar Crust

Peanut Brittle Pie

1 unbaked (9-inch) Stir-n-Roll Pie Crust (recipe follows)
1 cup beer nuts
3 eggs, at room temperature
3 tablespoons cornstarch
1 cup firmly packed light brown sugar
3 tablespoons WESSON® Corn Oil
1 cup maple syrup
1 teaspoon maple extract
1 teaspoon vanilla extract

Prepare Stir-n-Roll Pie Crust. Sprinkle bottom of crust with ½ cup nuts; set aside *remaining* nuts.

Preheat oven to 450°F. In a medium bowl, whisk eggs until foamy. In another medium bowl, gradually add eggs to cornstarch; mix well. Add brown sugar and Wesson Oil; blend well. Stir in maple syrup and extracts; mix well. Pour filling into nut-covered pie shell. Sprinkle *remaining* nuts on top. Bake at 450°F for 15 minutes. *Lower oven temperature to 350°F.* Continue baking for 30 minutes or until center has set. *Do not overbake.*
Makes 8 servings

STIR-N-ROLL PIE CRUST

1½ cups sifted all-purpose flour
¾ teaspoon salt
⅓ cup WESSON® Vegetable Oil
¼ cup ice water

In medium bowl, mix flour and salt. Add Wesson Oil and water all at once to flour. With a fork, stir until mixture holds together. Shape dough into a ball and flatten. Roll between two pieces of wax paper to a 12-inch diameter. Peel off one piece of paper and invert dough, paper side up, into 9-inch pie plate. Peel off second piece of paper. Ease and fit pastry into plate; trim and flute edges.
Makes one (9-inch) pie crust

With filling: Do not pierce pie crust. Fill as desired and bake according to pie recipe.

Baker's® One Bowl® Easy Chocolate Pecan Pie

4 squares BAKER'S® Semi-Sweet Baking Chocolate
2 tablespoons butter *or* margarine
1 unbaked deep-dish pastry shell (9-inch)
3 eggs, slightly beaten
1 cup corn syrup
¼ cup firmly packed light brown sugar
1 teaspoon vanilla
1½ cups pecan halves

HEAT oven to 350°F.

MICROWAVE chocolate and butter in large microwavable bowl on HIGH 1 to 2 minutes or until butter is melted. Stir until chocolate is completely melted.

BRUSH bottom of pastry shell with small amount of beaten egg. Stir eggs, corn syrup, sugar and vanilla into chocolate mixture until well blended. Stir in pecans. Pour into pastry shell.

BAKE 55 minutes or until knife inserted 2 inches from edge comes out clean. Cool on wire rack. Serve with COOL WHIP Whipped Topping, if desired.
Makes 8 servings

Chocolate Chunk Pecan Pie: Prepare as directed, stirring additional 4 squares BAKER'S® Semi-Sweet Baking Chocolate, coarsely chopped, into chocolate mixture along with pecans.

Melting Chocolate on Top of Stove: Melt chocolate and butter in 3-quart saucepan on very low heat; stir constantly until chocolate is just melted. Remove from heat. Continue as directed above.

Prep Time: 15 minutes
Bake Time: 55 minutes

To prevent corn syrup from sticking to the measuring cup, lightly spray the measuring cup with nonstick cooking spray before measuring.

Lemon Meringue Pie

....

1 cup graham cracker
    crumbs
¼ cup powdered sugar
2 tablespoons margarine,
    melted
1 tablespoon water
1½ cups granulated sugar,
    divided
⅓ cup cornstarch
1½ cups hot water
¼ cup cholesterol-free egg
    substitute
½ cup fresh lemon juice
1½ teaspoons grated lemon
    peel
3 egg whites
½ teaspoon vanilla
¼ teaspoon cream of tartar

1. Preheat oven to 375°F. Combine graham cracker crumbs and powdered sugar in small bowl. Stir in margarine and 1 tablespoon water; mix until crumbs are moistened. Press crumb mixture onto bottom and up side of 9-inch pie plate. Bake 6 to 9 minutes or until edges are golden brown. Cool on wire rack. *Reduce oven temperature to 350°F.*

2. Combine ½ cup granulated sugar and cornstarch in medium saucepan over low heat. Gradually stir in hot water until smooth. Add egg substitute. Bring to a boil, stirring constantly with wire whisk. Boil 1 minute. Remove from heat; stir in lemon juice and lemon peel. Pour hot filling into cooled crust.

3. Beat egg whites, vanilla and cream of tartar in large bowl until soft peaks form. Gradually add remaining 1 cup granulated sugar, beating until stiff peaks form. Spread meringue over filling, sealing carefully to edge of crust.

4. Bake 12 to 15 minutes or until meringue is golden brown. Cool to room temperature before serving.

Makes 8 servings

To obtain the fullest volume when beating egg whites, make sure the bowl and beaters are clean and dry. Never use a plastic bowl because it may retain an oily film even after repeated washings.

Lemon Meringue Pie

Caramel Apple Cupcakes

1 package butter-recipe yellow cake mix plus ingredients to prepare
1 cup chopped dried apples
  Caramel Frosting (recipe follows)
  Chopped nuts (optional)

1. Preheat oven to 375°F. Line 24 regular-size (2½-inch) muffin pan cups with paper muffin cup liners.

2. Prepare cake mix according to package directions. Stir in apples. Spoon batter into prepared muffin pans.

3. Bake 15 to 20 minutes or until toothpick inserted into centers comes out clean. Cool in pans on wire racks 10 minutes. Remove to racks; cool completely.

4. Prepare Caramel Frosting. Frost cupcakes. Sprinkle cupcakes with nuts, if desired.
Makes 24 cupcakes

CARAMEL FROSTING

3 tablespoons butter
1 cup packed brown sugar
½ cup evaporated milk
⅛ teaspoon salt
3¾ cups powdered sugar
¾ teaspoon vanilla

1. Melt butter in 2-quart saucepan. Stir in brown sugar, evaporated milk and salt. Bring to a boil, stirring constantly. Remove from heat; cool to lukewarm.

2. Beat in powdered sugar until frosting is of spreading consistency. Blend in vanilla.

Caramel Apple Cupcakes

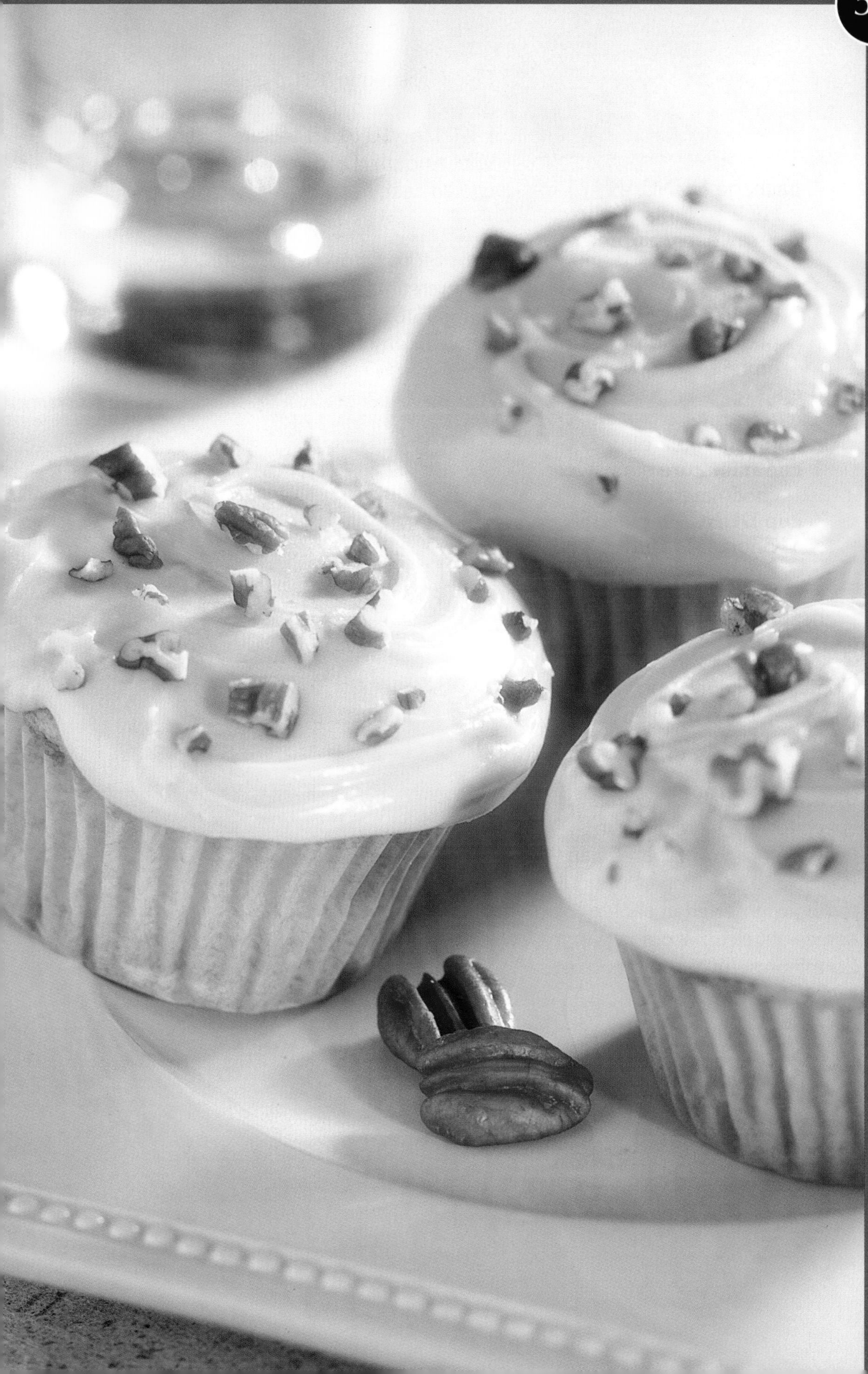

Strawberry Pound Cake

1 package DUNCAN HINES® Moist Deluxe Strawberry Supreme Cake Mix
1 (4-serving size) package vanilla-flavor instant pudding and pie filling mix
4 eggs
1 cup water
⅓ cup vegetable oil
1 cup miniature semisweet chocolate chips
⅔ cup DUNCAN HINES® Chocolate Butter Cream Frosting

Preheat oven to 350°F. Grease and flour 10-inch Bundt pan.

Combine cake mix, pudding mix, eggs, water and oil in large mixing bowl. Beat at low speed with electric mixer until moistened. Beat at medium speed for 2 minutes. Stir in chips. Pour into prepared pan. Bake 55 to 60 minutes or until toothpick inserted in center comes out clean. Cool in pan 25 minutes. Invert onto cooling rack. Cool completely.

Place frosting in 1-cup glass measuring cup. Microwave at HIGH for 10 to 15 seconds. Stir until smooth. Drizzle over top of cooled cake.

Makes 12 to 16 servings

Tip: Store leftover chocolate buttercream frosting, covered, in refrigerator. Spread frosting between graham crackers for a quick snack.

If it is difficult to test deep cakes (such as Bundt or tube cakes) for doneness with a toothpick, try using a wooden skewer or an uncooked spaghetti noodle.

Strawberry Pound Cake

Southern Jam Cake

CAKE
- ¾ cup butter or margarine, softened
- 1 cup granulated sugar
- 3 eggs
- 1 cup (12-ounce jar) SMUCKER'S® Seedless Blackberry Jam
- 2½ cups all-purpose flour
- 1 teaspoon baking soda
- 1 teaspoon ground cinnamon
- 1 teaspoon ground cloves
- 1 teaspoon ground allspice
- 1 teaspoon ground nutmeg
- ¾ cup buttermilk

CARAMEL ICING (OPTIONAL)
- 2 tablespoons butter
- ½ cup firmly packed brown sugar
- 3 tablespoons milk
- 1¾ cups powdered sugar

Grease and flour tube pan. Combine ¾ cup butter and granulated sugar; beat until light and fluffy. Add eggs one at a time, beating well after each addition. Fold in jam.

Combine flour, baking soda, cinnamon, cloves, allspice and nutmeg; mix well. Add to batter alternately with buttermilk, stirring just enough to blend after each addition. Spoon mixture into prepared pan.

Bake at 350°F for 50 minutes or until toothpick inserted in center comes out clean. Cool in pan for 10 minutes. Remove from pan; cool completely.

In saucepan, melt 2 tablespoons butter; stir in brown sugar. Cook, stirring constantly, until mixture boils; remove from heat. Cool 5 minutes. Stir in milk; blend in powdered sugar. Frost cake.

Makes 12 to 16 servings

Soured milk can be substituted for buttermilk. To sour milk: for each cup of buttermilk called for in the recipe, put 1 tablespoon lemon juice or white vinegar in a measuring cup and add enough milk to measure 1 cup. Stir and let stand for 5 minutes before using.

Pumpkin Spice Sheet Cake with Cream Cheese Frosting

2 cups granulated sugar
1 (16-ounce) can pumpkin
1 cup vegetable oil
4 eggs
2 cups all-purpose flour
2 teaspoons baking soda
1 teaspoon ground cinnamon
1 teaspoon pumpkin pie spice
½ teaspoon salt
4 ounces Neufchâtel or other low-fat cream cheese
¼ cup butter or margarine, softened
1 teaspoon vanilla extract
1¾ cups powdered sugar, sifted
1 tablespoon milk
¼ cup chopped pecans (optional)

Preheat oven to 350°F. Combine granulated sugar, pumpkin, oil and eggs in large bowl; mix well. Add flour, baking soda, cinnamon, pumpkin pie spice and salt; mix until well blended. Pour into greased 15×10×1-inch jelly roll pan. Bake 25 to 30 minutes or until toothpick inserted into center comes out clean. Set aside to cool. To prepare frosting, combine Neufchâtel cheese, butter and vanilla in large bowl; mix well. Blend in powdered sugar. Stir in milk until frosting is of spreading consistency. Frost cake and sprinkle with nuts, if desired.
Makes 15 to 20 servings

Favorite recipe from
Bob Evans®

To transport a cake to a bake sale without ruining the frosting, arrange several toothpicks or uncooked spaghetti noodles in the top of the cake before covering it with foil or plastic wrap. This will prevent the wrap from sticking to the frosting.

Take-Along Cake

- 1 package DUNCAN HINES® Moist Deluxe® Swiss Chocolate Cake Mix
- 1 (12-ounce) package semisweet chocolate chips
- 1 cup miniature marshmallows
- ¼ cup butter or margarine, melted
- ½ cup packed brown sugar
- ½ cup chopped pecans or walnuts

Preheat oven to 350°F. Grease and flour 13×9-inch pan.

Prepare cake mix as directed on package. Add chips and marshmallows to batter. Pour into prepared pan. Drizzle melted butter over batter. Sprinkle with sugar and top with pecans. Bake 45 to 55 minutes or until toothpick inserted in center comes out clean. Serve warm or cool completely in pan.

Makes 12 to 16 servings

Tip: To keep leftover pecans fresh, store them in the freezer in an airtight container.

Ice Cream Cone Cupcakes

- 1 package (18¼ ounces) white cake mix plus ingredients to prepare
- 2 tablespoons nonpareils
- 2 packages (1¾ ounces each) flat-bottomed ice cream cones (about 24 cones)
- 1 container (16 ounces) prepared vanilla or chocolate frosting
  Candies and other decorations

1. Preheat oven to 350°F.

2. Prepare cake mix according to package directions. Stir in nonpareils.

3. Spoon ¼ cup batter into each ice cream cone.

4. Stand cones on cookie sheet. Bake cones until toothpick inserted into centers comes out clean, about 20 minutes. Cool on wire racks.

5. Frost each filled cone. Decorate as desired.

Makes 24 cupcakes

Note: Cupcakes are best served the day they are prepared. Store loosely covered.

Ice Cream Cone Cupcakes

Baker's® One Bowl® Chocolate Cake

....

6 squares BAKER'S® Semi-
    Sweet Baking
    Chocolate
¾ cup (1½ sticks) butter *or*
    margarine
1½ cups sugar
3 eggs
2 teaspoons vanilla
2½ cups all-purpose flour
1 teaspoon baking soda
¼ teaspoon salt
1½ cups water

HEAT oven to 350°F. Grease and flour 2 (9-inch) round cake pans.

MICROWAVE chocolate and butter in large microwavable bowl on HIGH 2 minutes or until butter is melted. Stir until chocolate is completely melted.

STIR sugar into chocolate mixture. Beat in eggs, one at a time, with electric mixer on low speed until completely mixed. Add vanilla. Add ½ cup of the flour, baking soda and salt. Beat in the remaining 2 cups flour alternately with water until well blended. Pour into prepared pans.

BAKE 35 minutes or until toothpick inserted into center comes out clean. Cool 10 minutes; remove from pans. Cool completely on wire racks. Fill and frost layers with Baker's® One Bowl® Chocolate Frosting (page 60), or as desired.

Makes 12 servings

Prep Time: 15 minutes
Bake Time: 35 minutes

Black Forest Cake (as shown): Mix 1 can (21 ounces) cherry pie filling, drained, and ¼ cup cherry liqueur (or ½ teaspoon almond extract). Spoon evenly over 1 cake layer, reserving a few cherries for garnish, if desired. Spread 1½ cups thawed COOL WHIP Whipped Topping over cherries; top with second cake layer. Frost top and sides with additional 2 cups whipped topping. Garnish as desired. Refrigerate.

Black Forest Cake

Baker's® One Bowl® Chocolate Frosting

1 package (8 squares)
   BAKER'S® Semi-Sweet
   Baking Chocolate
1 package (16 ounces)
   powdered sugar (about
   4 cups)
½ cup (1 stick) butter *or*
   margarine, softened
2 teaspoons vanilla
⅓ cup milk

MICROWAVE chocolate in large microwavable bowl on HIGH 1 to 2 minutes. Stir until chocolate is melted and smooth. Cool for five minutes or to room temperature.

ADD sugar, butter and vanilla. Gradually beat in milk with electric mixer on low speed until well blended. If frosting becomes too thick, beat in additional milk by teaspoonfuls until of spreading consistency.

Makes 3 cups or enough to frost tops and sides of 2 (8- or 9-inch) cake layers or top and sides of a 13×9-inch cake or tops of 3 (8- or 9-inch) cake layers or 18 to 24 cupcakes

Prep Time: 10 minutes

6 ingredients or less!

Angel Almond Cupcakes

1 package DUNCAN
   HINES® Angel Food
   Cake Mix
1¼ cups water
2 teaspoons almond
   extract
1 container DUNCAN
   HINES® Wild Cherry
   Vanilla Frosting

Preheat oven to 350°F.

Combine cake mix, water and almond extract in large mixing bowl. Beat at low speed with electric mixer until moistened. Beat at medium speed for 1 minute. Line medium muffin pans with paper baking cups. Fill muffin cups two-thirds full. Bake 20 to 25 minutes or until golden brown, cracked and dry. Remove from muffin pans. Cool completely. Frost with frosting.

Makes 30 to 32 cupcakes

Angel Almond Cupcakes

Banana Split Cupcakes

1 (18¼ ounces) yellow
    cake mix, divided
1 cup mashed ripe bananas
1 cup water
3 eggs
1 cup chopped drained
    maraschino cherries
1½ cups miniature semi-
    sweet chocolate chips,
    divided
1½ cups prepared vanilla
    frosting
1 cup marshmallow creme
1 teaspoon shortening
30 whole maraschino
    cherries, drained and
    patted dry

1. Preheat oven to 350°F. Line 30 regular-size (2½-inch) muffin cups with paper muffin cup liners.

2. Reserve 2 tablespoons cake mix. Combine remaining cake mix, bananas, water and eggs in large bowl. Beat at low speed of electric mixer until moistened, about 30 seconds. Beat at medium speed 2 minutes. Combine chopped cherries and reserved cake mix in small bowl. Stir chopped cherry mixture and 1 cup chocolate chips into batter.

3. Spoon batter into prepared muffin cups. Bake 15 to 20 minutes or until toothpick inserted in centers comes out clean. Cool in pans on wire racks 10 minutes. Remove to wire racks; cool completely.

4. Combine frosting and marshmallow creme in medium bowl until well blended. Frost each cupcake with frosting mixture.

5. Combine remaining ½ cup chocolate chips and shortening in small microwavable bowl. Microwave at HIGH 30 to 45 seconds, stirring after 30 seconds, or until smooth. Drizzle chocolate mixture over cupcakes. Place one whole cherry on each cupcake.

Makes 30 cupcakes

Note: If desired, omit chocolate drizzle and top cupcakes with colored sprinkles.

Banana Split Cupcakes

BREAD WINNERS

Cranberry Cheesecake Muffins

1 package (3 ounces)
    cream cheese, softened
4 tablespoons sugar,
    divided
1 cup reduced-fat (2%)
    milk
⅓ cup vegetable oil
1 egg
1 package (15.6 ounces)
    cranberry quick bread
    mix

1. Preheat oven to 400°F. Grease 12 muffin cups.

2. Beat cream cheese and 2 tablespoons sugar in small bowl until well blended.

3. Beat milk, oil and egg in large bowl until blended. Stir in quick bread mix just until moistened.

4. Fill muffin cups ¼ full with batter. Drop 1 teaspoon cream cheese mixture into center of each cup. Spoon remaining batter over cream cheese mixture.

5. Sprinkle batter with remaining 2 tablespoons sugar. Bake 17 to 22 minutes or until golden brown. Cool 5 minutes. Remove from muffin cups to wire rack to cool.
Makes 12 muffins

Do not overmix muffin batter. Too much stirring will give muffins a tough texture with peaked tops and lots of holes and tunnels. The batter should look lumpy when it goes into the prepared muffin pans.

Cranberry Cheesecake Muffins

Orange Chocolate Chip Bread

½ cup nonfat milk
½ cup plain nonfat yogurt
⅓ cup sugar
¼ cup orange juice
1 egg, slightly beaten
1 tablespoon freshly grated orange peel
3 cups all-purpose biscuit baking mix
½ cup HERSHEY'S MINI CHIPS™ Semi-Sweet Chocolate

1. Heat oven to 350°F. Grease 9×5×3-inch loaf pan or spray with vegetable cooking spray.

2. Stir together milk, yogurt, sugar, orange juice, egg and orange peel in large bowl; add baking mix. With spoon, beat until well blended, about 1 minute. Stir in small chocolate chips. Pour into prepared pan.

3. Bake 45 to 50 minutes or until wooden pick inserted in center comes out clean. Cool 10 minutes; remove from pan to wire rack. Cool completely before slicing. Garnish as desired. Wrap leftover bread in foil or plastic wrap. Store at room temperature or freeze for longer storage.

Makes 1 loaf (16 slices)

Apple Orchard Bread

WESSON® No-Stick Cooking Spray
4 cups diced peeled Fuji or Red Delicious apples
½ cup WESSON® Vegetable Oil
3 eggs
2 cups all-purpose flour
1½ cups packed brown sugar
1 cup chopped nuts
2 teaspoons baking soda
1½ teaspoons ground cinnamon
¾ teaspoon salt

Preheat oven to 325°F. Grease two 8½×4½×2½-inch loaf pans with Wesson Cooking Spray; set aside. In mixing bowl, combine apples, Wesson Oil and eggs until well blended. Mix in flour, sugar, nuts, baking soda, cinnamon and salt; blend well. (Batter will be very thick.) Evenly divide batter into prepared pans. Bake 1 hour or until wooden pick inserted into center comes out clean; cool.

Makes 2 loaves

Preparation Time: 15 minutes
Baking Time: 1 hour

Orange Chocolate Chip Bread

Raspberry-Applesauce Coffee Cake

1½ cups fresh or frozen
    raspberries
¼ cup water
7 tablespoons sugar,
    divided
2 tablespoons cornstarch
½ teaspoon ground
    nutmeg, divided
1¾ cups all-purpose flour,
    divided
3 tablespoons margarine
1 tablespoon finely
    chopped walnuts
1½ teaspoons baking
    powder
½ teaspoon baking soda
⅛ teaspoon ground cloves
2 egg whites
1 cup unsweetened
    applesauce

Preheat oven to 350°F. Spray 8-inch square baking pan with nonstick cooking spray.

Combine raspberries and water in small saucepan; bring to a boil over high heat. Reduce heat to medium. Combine 2 tablespoons sugar, cornstarch and ¼ teaspoon nutmeg in small bowl. Stir into raspberry mixture. Cook and stir until mixture boils and thickens. Cook and stir 2 minutes more.

Combine ¾ cup flour and remaining 5 tablespoons sugar in medium bowl. Cut in margarine with pastry blender until mixture resembles coarse meal. Set aside ½ cup mixture for topping; stir walnuts into remaining crumb mixture.

Add remaining 1 cup flour, baking powder, baking soda, remaining ¼ teaspoon nutmeg and cloves to walnut mixture; mix well. Stir in egg whites and applesauce; beat until well combined. Spread half of batter into prepared pan. Spread raspberry mixture over batter. Drop remaining batter in small mounds on top. Sprinkle with reserved topping.

Bake 40 to 45 minutes or until edges start to pull away from sides of pan. Serve warm or cool. *Makes 9 servings*

Raspberry-Applesauce
Coffee Cake

Pumpkin Maple Cream Cheese Muffins

CREAM CHEESE FILLING

4 ounces cream cheese, softened

2 tablespoons packed brown sugar

1½ teaspoons maple flavoring

MUFFINS

2 cups all-purpose flour

¾ cup packed brown sugar

½ cup chopped walnuts

2 teaspoons baking powder

1 teaspoon ground cinnamon

½ teaspoon baking soda

¼ teaspoon salt

1 cup LIBBY'S® Solid Pack Pumpkin

¾ cup CARNATION® Evaporated Milk

2 eggs

¼ cup vegetable oil

2 teaspoons maple flavoring

Nut Topping (recipe follows)

FOR CREAM CHEESE FILLING

COMBINE cream cheese, 2 tablespoons brown sugar and 1½ teaspoons maple flavoring in small bowl until blended.

FOR MUFFINS

COMBINE flour, ¾ cup brown sugar, walnuts, baking powder, cinnamon, baking soda and salt in large bowl. Combine pumpkin, evaporated milk, eggs, oil and 2 teaspoons maple flavoring; mix well. Add pumpkin mixture to flour mixture, mixing just until blended.

SPOON into 12 greased or paper-lined muffin cups (cups will be very full). Dollop 1 heaping teaspoon of Cream Cheese Filling into center of each cup, pressing into batter slightly. Sprinkle Nut Topping over muffins.

BAKE in preheated 400°F. oven for 20 to 25 minutes or until wooden pick inserted in center comes out clean. Cool in pan for 5 minutes; remove to wire rack to cool completely.

Makes 12 muffins

Nut Topping: Combine 2 tablespoons packed brown sugar and ¼ cup chopped walnuts in small bowl.

Blueberry Kuchen

1½ cups all-purpose flour
2 teaspoons baking
   powder
½ cup EGG BEATERS®
   Healthy Real Egg
   Product
⅓ cup skim milk
1 teaspoon vanilla extract
½ cup granulated sugar
¼ cup FLEISCHMANN'S®
   Original Margarine,
   softened
1 (21-ounce) can blueberry
   pie filling and topping
   Streusel Topping (recipe
   follows)
   Powdered Sugar Glaze,
   optional (recipe
   follows)

In small bowl, combine flour and baking powder; set aside. In another small bowl, combine Egg Beaters®, milk and vanilla; set aside.

In medium bowl, with electric mixer at medium speed, beat granulated sugar and margarine until creamy. Alternately add flour mixture and egg mixture, blending well after each addition. Spread batter into greased 9-inch square baking pan.

Bake at 350°F for 20 minutes. Spoon blueberry pie filling over batter; sprinkle Streusel Topping over filling. Bake for 10 to 15 minutes more or until toothpick inserted in center comes out clean. Cool in pan on wire rack. Drizzle with Powdered Sugar Glaze, if desired. Cut into 12 (3×2-inch) pieces.

Makes 12 servings

Streusel Topping: In small bowl, combine 3 tablespoons all-purpose flour, 3 tablespoons powdered sugar and ¼ teaspoon ground cinnamon. Cut in 1 tablespoon Fleischmann's Original Margarine until crumbly.

Powdered Sugar Glaze: In small bowl, combine 1 cup powdered sugar and 5 to 6 teaspoons water until smooth.

Prep Time: 20 minutes
Bake Time: 35 minutes

Lemon Poppy Seed Tea Loaf

TEA LOAF

2½ cups all-purpose flour
¼ cup poppy seeds
1 tablespoon grated lemon
    peel
2 teaspoons baking
    powder
½ teaspoon baking soda
½ teaspoon salt
1 cup sugar
⅔ cup MOTT'S® Natural
    Apple Sauce
1 whole egg
2 egg whites, lightly beaten
2 tablespoons vegetable oil
1 teaspoon vanilla extract
⅓ cup skim milk

LEMON SYRUP

¼ cup sugar
¼ cup lemon juice

1. Preheat oven to 350°F. Spray 9×5-inch loaf pan with nonstick cooking spray.

2. To prepare Tea Loaf, in large bowl, combine flour, poppy seeds, lemon peel, baking powder, baking soda and salt.

3. In medium bowl, combine 1 cup sugar, apple sauce, whole egg, egg whites, oil and vanilla.

4. Stir apple sauce mixture into flour mixture alternately with milk. Mix until thoroughly moistened. Spread batter into prepared pan.

5. Bake 40 to 45 minutes or until toothpick inserted in center comes out clean. Cool in pan 10 minutes. Invert onto wire rack; turn right side up.

6. To prepare Lemon Syrup, in small saucepan, combine ¼ cup sugar and lemon juice. Cook, stirring frequently, until sugar dissolves. Cool slightly.

7. Pierce top of loaf with metal skewer. Brush lemon syrup over loaf. Let stand until cool. Cut into 16 slices.

Makes 16 servings

Before grating lemon peel, be sure to scrub the lemon with warm, soapy water to remove wax and any traces of insecticide.

Left to right: Lemon Poppy Seed Tea Loaf and Morning Glory Bread (page 76)

Tropical Treat Muffins

· ·

2 cups all-purpose flour
⅓ cup plus 1 tablespoon sugar, divided
1 tablespoon baking powder
1 teaspoon grated lemon peel
½ teaspoon salt
¾ cup (4 ounces) dried papaya, finely diced
½ cup coarsely chopped banana chips
½ cup chopped macadamia nuts
¼ cup flaked coconut
½ cup milk
½ cup butter, melted
¼ cup sour cream
1 egg, beaten

Preheat oven to 400°F. Grease or paper-line 12 (2½-inch) or 6 (4-inch) large muffin cups.

Combine flour, ⅓ cup sugar, baking powder, lemon peel and salt in large bowl. Combine papaya, banana chips, macadamia nuts and coconut in small bowl; stir in 1 tablespoon flour mixture until well coated.

Combine milk, butter, sour cream and egg in another small bowl until blended; stir into flour mixture just until moistened. Fold in fruit mixture. Spoon evenly into prepared muffin cups. Sprinkle remaining 1 tablespoon sugar over tops of muffins.

Bake 15 to 20 minutes for regular-size muffins, 25 to 30 minutes for jumbo muffins, or until wooden pick inserted in center comes out clean. Remove from pan. Cool on wire rack.

Makes 12 regular-size or 6 jumbo muffins

Combining fruits and nuts with a small amount of the flour from the recipe before adding them to the batter prevents them from sinking to the bottoms of the muffins.

Tropical Treat Muffins

Morning Glory Bread

2½ cups all-purpose flour
2 teaspoons baking powder
1 teaspoon baking soda
½ teaspoon salt
½ teaspoon ground cinnamon
¼ teaspoon ground nutmeg
¼ teaspoon ground allspice
¾ cup granulated sugar
¾ cup firmly packed light brown sugar
½ cup MOTT'S® Chunky Apple Sauce
3 egg whites
1 tablespoon vegetable oil
1 tablespoon GRANDMA'S® Molasses
¾ cup finely shredded carrots
½ cup raisins
⅓ cup drained, crushed pineapple in juice
¼ cup shredded coconut

1. Preheat oven to 375°F. Spray 8½×4½-inch loaf pan with nonstick cooking spray.

2. In large bowl, combine flour, baking powder, baking soda, salt, cinnamon, nutmeg and allspice.

3. In medium bowl, combine granulated sugar, brown sugar, apple sauce, egg whites, oil and molasses.

4. Stir apple sauce mixture into flour mixture just until moistened. Fold in carrots, raisins, pineapple and coconut. Spread into prepared pan.

5. Bake 45 to 50 minutes or until toothpick inserted in center comes out clean. Cool in pan 10 minutes. Invert onto wire rack; turn right side up. Cool completely. Cut into 16 slices.

Makes 16 servings

To soften raisins that have become extremely hard during storage, place ½ cup of raisins in a 1-cup microwavable bowl. Cover with water and heat at HIGH 2 to 2½ minutes. Allow to stand 3 to 5 minutes; drain.

6 ingredients or less!

Nutty Blueberry Muffins

1 package DUNCAN HINES® Blueberry Muffin Mix
2 egg whites
⅓ cup water
⅓ cup chopped pecans

Preheat oven to 400°F. Grease 2½-inch muffin cups (or use paper liners).

Rinse blueberries from mix with cold water and drain.

Pour muffin mix into large bowl. Break up any lumps. Add egg whites and water. Stir until moistened, about 50 strokes. Stir in pecans; fold in blueberries.

For large muffins, fill cups two-thirds full. Bake 17 to 22 minutes or until toothpick inserted in center comes out clean. (For medium muffins, fill cups half full. Bake 15 to 20 minutes.) Cool in pan 5 to 10 minutes. Loosen carefully before removing from pan.

Makes 8 large or 12 medium muffins

Tip: To reheat leftover muffins, wrap the muffins tightly in foil. Place them in a 400°F oven for 10 to 15 minutes.

It is important to gently fold in blueberries when adding them to a batter. Vigorous stirring can rupture the berries, causing the batter to become blue.

Walnut Cheddar Apple Bread

½ cup butter, softened
1 cup packed light brown
    sugar
2 eggs
1 teaspoon vanilla
2 cups all-purpose flour
2 teaspoons baking
    powder
1 teaspoon baking soda
¼ teaspoon salt
1 cup sour cream
¼ cup milk
1 cup (4 ounces) shredded
    Cheddar cheese
1 cup diced dried apple
½ cup coarsely chopped
    walnuts

Preheat oven to 350°F. Grease 9×5-inch loaf pan.

Beat butter and sugar in large bowl with electric mixer on medium speed until light and fluffy. Beat in eggs and vanilla until blended. Combine flour, baking powder, baking soda and salt in small bowl. Add flour mixture to butter mixture on low speed alternately with sour cream and milk, beginning and ending with flour mixture; mix well after each addition. Stir in cheese, apples and walnuts. Spoon batter into prepared pan.

Bake 50 to 55 minutes or until wooden pick inserted in center comes out clean. Cool in pan 15 minutes. Remove from pan and cool completely on wire rack. Store tightly wrapped in plastic wrap at room temperature.

Makes 1 loaf

Alternately adding the flour and liquid ingredients limits the amount of time the flour proteins are exposed to liquid, creating a more tender quick bread.

Walnut Cheddar Apple Bread

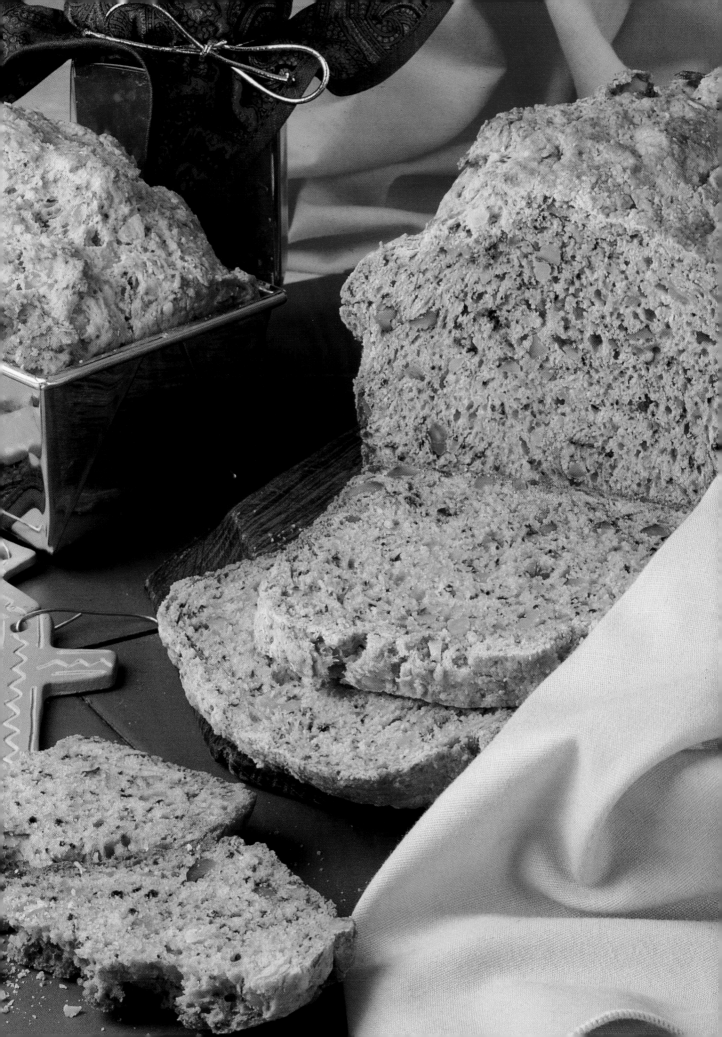

6 ingredients or less!

Fudgy Banana Rocky Road Clusters

1 package (12 ounces)
    semisweet chocolate
    chips (2 cups)
⅓ cup peanut butter
3 cups miniature
    marshmallows
1 cup unsalted peanuts
1 cup banana chips

Line baking sheets with waxed paper. Grease waxed paper.

Place chocolate chips and peanut butter in large microwave-safe bowl. Microwave at HIGH 2 minutes or until chips are melted and mixture is smooth, stirring twice. Fold in marshmallows, peanuts and banana chips.

Drop rounded tablespoonfuls candy mixture onto prepared baking sheets; refrigerate until firm. Store in airtight container in refrigerator.

Makes 2½ to 3 dozen clusters

Tip: If you prefer more nuts, use chunky peanut butter.

Storing marshmallows in the freezer will prevent them from drying out and becoming hard.

Fudgy Banana Rocky
Road Clusters

Cashew & Pretzel Toffee Clusters

¾ cup packed brown sugar
¾ cup light corn syrup
½ cup butter
2 teaspoons vanilla
4 cups tiny pretzel twists (not sticks)
4 cups bite-sized toasted wheat squares cereal
1 can (10 ounces) salted cashew halves and pieces

1. Preheat oven to 300°F. Spray large baking sheet with nonstick cooking spray.

2. Place sugar, syrup and butter in heavy small saucepan. Heat over medium heat until mixture boils and sugar dissolves, stirring frequently. Remove from heat; stir in vanilla.

3. Combine pretzels, cereal and cashews in large bowl. Pour sugar mixture over pretzel mixture; toss to coat evenly. Spread on prepared baking sheet. Bake 30 minutes, stirring after 15 minutes. Spread onto greased waxed paper. Cool completely; break into clusters. Store in airtight container at room temperature.

Makes about 8 cups clusters

6 ingredients or less!

Coconut Honey Pop Corn Balls

3 quarts popped JOLLY TIME® Pop Corn
¾ cup coconut
⅓ cup honey
½ teaspoon ground cinnamon
Dash of salt
3 tablespoons butter or margarine

Preheat oven to 250°F. Line shallow pan with foil. Place popped pop corn in pan. Keep pop corn warm in oven. Spread coconut in shallow baking pan; toast coconut, stirring once, about 8 to 10 minutes. Combine honey, cinnamon and salt in small saucepan. Heat to boiling; boil 1½ minutes, stirring constantly. Add butter; stir until melted. Pour honey mixture over pop corn. Add coconut. Toss well. Cool just enough to handle. With Jolly Time® Pop Corn Ball Maker or buttered hands, shape into balls.

Makes about 10 pop corn balls

Cashew & Pretzel Toffee Clusters

Microwave Nut Brittle

MAZOLA NO STICK® Cooking Spray
1 cup sugar
½ cup KARO® Light Corn Syrup
⅛ teaspoon salt
1½ cups roasted peanuts, cashews or mixed nuts
1 teaspoon baking soda
1 teaspoon MAZOLA® Margarine or butter
1 teaspoon vanilla

1. Spray cookie sheet and metal spatula with cooking spray.

2. In 2-quart microwavable glass measuring cup or bowl, stir sugar, corn syrup and salt with wooden spoon until well mixed.

3. Microwave on High (100%) 7 to 8 minutes or until syrup is pale yellow. *(Candy syrup is very hot. Handle carefully; do not touch hot mixture.)*

4. Stir in nuts. Microwave on High 1 to 2 minutes or until nuts are lightly browned. Immediately stir in baking soda, margarine and vanilla until foamy.

5. Quickly pour onto cookie sheet; spread evenly with spatula. Cool; break into pieces. Store in tightly covered container.

Makes about 1¼ pounds

Microwave Candy Making Tips: Do not use plastic utensils. Bowl will be hot; use potholders. For easy cleanup, soak bowl and utensils in hot water.

Prep Time: 20 minutes, plus cooling

Do not store hard candies, like peanut brittle, with other candies. Moisture from soft candies will make hard candies sticky.

Peanut Butter Fudge

1 (16-ounce) box
   DOMINO® Light Brown
   Sugar (approximately
   2¼ cups)
½ cup milk
2 tablespoons butter
¾ cup peanut butter
½ cup chopped peanuts
1 teaspoon vanilla

Butter 9×5-inch loaf pan; set aside. Heat sugar, milk and butter in heavy 2-quart saucepan. Bring to a boil, stirring constantly until sugar is dissolved. Continue boiling 5 minutes longer, stirring constantly. Cool 10 minutes. Add peanut butter, peanuts and vanilla. Stir until well blended. Pour into prepared pan. Refrigerate at least 3 hours.

Makes about 27 candies

People Chow

1 cup butter or margarine
1 package (12 ounces)
   semisweet chocolate
   chips
18 cups dry cereal (mixture
   of bite-sized wheat,
   corn and rice cereal
   squares or toasted oat
   cereal)
2 cups nuts (cashews,
   peanuts, mixed nuts,
   pecans or walnuts)
6 cups powdered sugar

Melt butter and chocolate chips in heavy medium saucepan over low heat; stir to blend. Place cereal and nuts in large bowl. Pour chocolate mixture over; mix until cereal and nuts are thoroughly coated. Turn chocolate mixture into very large bowl or dishpan. Sprinkle sugar over, 2 cups at a time, carefully folding and mixing until thoroughly coated.

Makes about 24 cups

6 ingredients or less!

Caramel-Marshmallow Apples

1 package (14 ounces)
   caramels
1 cup miniature
   marshmallows
1 tablespoon water
5 or 6 small apples

1. Line baking sheet with buttered waxed paper; set aside.

2. Combine caramels, marshmallows and water in medium saucepan. Cook over medium heat, stirring constantly, until caramels melt. Cool slightly while preparing apples.

3. Rinse and thoroughly dry apples. Insert flat sticks in stem ends of apples.

4. Dip each apple in caramel mixture, coating apples. Remove excess caramel mixture by scraping apple bottoms across rim of saucepan. Place on prepared baking sheet. Refrigerate until firm.

Makes 5 or 6 apples

Caramel-Nut Apples: Roll coated apples in chopped nuts before refrigerating.

Caramel-Chocolate Apples: Drizzle melted milk chocolate over coated apples before refrigerating.

After the caramel has become firm, remove apples from the baking sheet and place in paper baking cups to serve, if desired.

Clockwise from left:
Caramel-Marshmallow Apple,
Caramel-Nut Apple and
Caramel-Chocolate Apple

Easy Turtle Fudge

1 package (12 ounces)
    semisweet chocolate
    chips (2 cups)
2 ounces bittersweet or
    semisweet chocolate,
    chopped
1 cup sweetened
    condensed milk
¼ teaspoon salt
30 caramel candies,
    unwrapped
1 tablespoon water
40 pecan halves

1. Grease 11×7-inch pan; set aside.

2. Melt chips in heavy medium saucepan over very low heat, stirring constantly. Remove from heat. Stir in bittersweet chocolate until melted. Stir in sweetened condensed milk and salt until smooth.

3. Spread in prepared pan; cover with foil. Refrigerate until firm.

4. Cut fudge into squares. Transfer to baking sheet lined with waxed paper.

5. Place caramels and water in heavy small saucepan. Heat over low heat until melted, stirring frequently. Drizzle or top fudge pieces with caramel mixture. Top each piece with 1 pecan half.

6. Store in airtight container in freezer. Bring to room temperature before serving.

Makes 40 candies

To make ahead, cut fudge into pieces, wrap and freeze for up to 6 months. Do not top with caramel or nuts. Thaw wrapped fudge at room temperature for about 3 hours. Drizzle with caramel and top with nuts as directed.

Easy Turtle Fudge

6 ingredients or less!

Butterscotch Rocky Road

1½ cups miniature
    marshmallows
1 cup coarsely chopped
    pecans
2 cups (12 ounces)
    butterscotch chips
½ cup sweetened
    condensed milk

1. Butter 13×9-inch pan.
Spread marshmallows and
pecans evenly on bottom of pan.

2. Melt butterscotch chips in
heavy, medium saucepan over
low heat, stirring constantly. Stir
in condensed milk.

3. Pour butterscotch mixture
over marshmallows and pecans,
covering entire mixture. If
necessary, use a knife or small
spatula to help cover the
marshmallows and nuts with
butterscotch mixture. Let stand
in pan until set.

4. Cut into squares. Store in
refrigerator.

Makes about 35 pieces

6 ingredients or less!

Chocolate Pecan Popcorn Bars

3 quarts popped corn
2 cups pecan halves or
    coarsely chopped
    pecans
2 cups (12 ounces)
    semisweet chocolate
    chips
¾ cup sugar
¾ cup KARO® Light or
    Dark Corn Syrup
2 tablespoons MAZOLA®
    Margarine

1. Preheat oven to 300°F. In
large roasting pan combine
popped corn and pecans.

2. In medium saucepan combine
chocolate chips, sugar, corn
syrup and margarine. Stirring
occasionally, bring to boil over
medium-high heat; boil 1 minute.
Pour over popcorn mixture; toss
to coat well.

3. Bake 30 minutes, stirring
twice.

4. Spoon into 13×9-inch baking
pan. Press warm mixture firmly
and evenly into pan. Cool 5
minutes. Invert onto cutting
board. Cut into bars.

Makes about 30 bars

ACKNOWLEDGMENTS

**The publisher would like to thank the companies
and organizations listed below for the use of their
recipes and photographs in this publication.**

Bestfoods

Bob Evans®

ConAgra Grocery Products Company

Dole Food Company, Inc.

Domino Sugar Corporation

Duncan Hines® and Moist Deluxe® are registered
trademarks of Aurora Foods Inc.

Egg Beaters®

Hershey Foods Corporation

JOLLY TIME® Pop Corn

Keebler Company

Kraft Foods, Inc.

M&M/MARS

MOTT'S® Inc., a division of Cadbury Beverages Inc.

Nabisco Biscuit Company

Nestlé USA, Inc.

OREO® Cookies

The Procter & Gamble Company

The Quaker® Oatmeal Kitchens

The J.M. Smucker Company

INDEX